Anne With An E

& Me

D1738665

ISBN 9781387475872

ALSO FROM PALOMA PRESS:

Blue by Wesley St. Jo & Remé Grefalda
Manhattan: An Archaeology by Eileen R. Tabios

FORTHCOMING IN 2018:

HUMANITY, An Anthology edited by Eileen R. Tabios
Humors by Joel Chace
My Beauty is an Occupiable Space by Anne Gorrick & John
    Bloomberg-Rissman
peminology[i] by Melinda Luisa de Jesús

PALOMA PRESS

Publishing Poetry+Prose with Panache since 2016
www.palomapress.net

ANNE WITH AN E & ME

Wesley St. Jo

Paloma Press, 2018

Anne of Green Gables (1908)

CONTENTS

"Kindred spirits are not so scarce as I used to think. It's splendid to find out there are so many of them in the world."

—Anne Shirley in *Anne of Green Gables* by L. M. Montgomery

For my sister and kindred spirit

1

"*There's such a lot of different Annes in me. I sometimes think that is why I'm such a troublesome person. If I was just the one Anne it would be ever so much more comfortable, but then it wouldn't be half so interesting.*" —*A.S.*

CLARITY

I wish to begin
the year
with clarity—
my favorite word
next to
epiphany.
I shall be
friends with Cindy and Meg
and smile charmingly at Anthony.
(Will he walk me to class?
Kiss me, perhaps?)

I wish to join a club,
run track,
and someday, be
Homecoming Queen
(needless to say,
I will get
a 4.0 GPA)!

I shall learn
to speak
perfect Pashto
(find some use for it
when I'm an astronaut
and sometimes swathed
in wild indigo).

But first,
I shall begin
this year
with Clarity.
Like Komorebi,
which is what
I truly hope
to be:

"*light filtering through trees.*"

2

"Well, that is another hope gone. 'My life is a
perfect graveyard of buried hopes.' That's a
sentence I read in a book once, and I say it over
to comfort myself whenever I'm disappointed in
anything." —A.S.

BROKEN HEART

Have you ever heard
a heart break?
It's like a star whale
in agony—
an opening
hewn on its head,
forced to ferry
a ship on its back.

It is also the sound
of his voice as he
speaks to her,
and to you of her.
O heart,
break,
or don't break.
I think I will
forever
hear his voice
with an ache.

3

"Oh, look, here's a big bee just tumbled out of an apple blossom. Just think what a lovely place to live—in an apple blossom! Fancy going to sleep in it when the wind was rocking it. If I wasn't a human girl, I think I'd like to be a bee and live among the flowers."—A.S.

TESSALATIONS

Finding pentaminoes
is all about possibilities.
You've got a puzzle?
Learn the pattern!
Flip,
Rotate,
Tessalate!
In the Game of Life,
the smallest unit
is only as good as
its eight neighbors:
2 or 3 good ones
and it lives;
but 4 or more
and it will give.

4

"Which would you rather be if you had the choice–divinely beautiful or dazzlingly clever or angelically good?" —A.S.

HAIR

It's a bad hair day.
The frizz just won't be tamed
and I'm running late.
Shall I braid
my hair like yours?

It's a bad hair day.
(By the way,
did you know
that you're "Carrots"
because of pheomelanin?
Mine's a plain brown mane
because of eumelanin.
At least Xie Qiuping's
is darker and finer,
though I can't imagine
not cutting my hair
for 31 years or longer.)

Someday you'll be an
auburn-haired legend,
as lovely as
any Gibson beauty.
But will I always be a
garden-variety,
brown-haired,
brown-eyed,

not-pretty-not-ugly,
hippie?

It's a bad hair day.
Think I'll just wear a beanie.
Between that and my
certified geek status,
nobody would care.

Not my cat, Mr. Sassafras,

or any of the boys

in my class.

5

"*It is ever so much easier to be good if your clothes are fashionable.*"—A.S.

JUICY

My best friend loves to shop
at the mall,

on eBay and other online layaways.
She looks for what she adores.

She doesn't care
what people call
people like her.
Says she's not a shopaholic,
she just likes nice things, you see.

Hats, bags, tees, and all kinds of goodies
Necklace, shoes, pants, and panties
Pinks, browns, blues, and greens
You name it, she's got it.

Outlets are her favorite thing,
"Clearance sale" is the magic word to begin.
Give her used items as long as it's PRADA.
Throw in Burberry, Tiffany, Mulberry,
Chanel, LV, Juicy, yada, yada, yada.

She's always on the lookout
for something unique,
something she can afford,
something she can hoard.

Like Pippa Middleton,
she'd buy a MilliMillu creation
and Swarovskis at an auction.

6

"It has always seemed to me, ever since early childhood, amid all the commonplaces of life, I was very near to a kingdom of ideal beauty. Between it and me hung only a thin veil. I could never draw it quite aside, but sometimes a wind fluttered it and I caught a glimpse of the enchanting realms beyond-only a glimpse-but those glimpses have always made life worthwhile." —A.S.

The Ancient
Mariner lamp twinkled
and sailed,
bringing her to Old
Avonlea.

Its dim blue light
danced in the
shadows, drawing
images on the wall
of treacherous
seas and sunken ships,
and lost sailors.

The lamp
boasted scenes from
bygone
generations,
of a peculiar girl
with the flaming
hair.

From the light of
the lamp came
ghostly
mirages of sea
creatures and murals of
drunken pyrates
on a perilous
voyage.

Fragments of sea
life burst
into view as the final
flicker of light
from the tired
old lamp faded.
In the daylight,
there was no flaming
hair. Just a peculiar

girl in the bleachers.

7

"People laugh at me because I use big words. But if you have big ideas, you have to use big words to express them, haven't you?"
—A.S.

SOCKDOLAGER

—for Eileen Tabios

I can't believe
she just
honeyfuggled

that jimberjawed mollagausauger!
Bet she
didn't

mean to hornswoggle.
It's a
sockdolager!

8

"*Dear old world, you are very lovely, and I am glad to be alive in you.*" —A.S.

ANNE'S SONG

Île-du-Prince-Édouard,
Prince Edward Island,

Eilean a' Phrionnsa,
The Island of the Prince,

Abegweit,
land cradled in the waves,

Garden of the Gulf,
home to red sandstone cliffs,

silica sand, singing sands,
saltwater marshes and

shifting dunes,
red foxes and blue jays,

piping plovers and robins,
Green Gables and Gil.

The text visible within the illustration (book cover): "Anne with an E and me"

9

"I read in a book once that a rose by any other name would smell as sweet, but I've never been able to believe it. I don't believe a rose WOULD be as nice if it was called a thistle or a skunk cabbage."
—A.S.

Pigsqueak prettily

spreads in the spring

its nodding clusters of
magenta-pink flowers.

Bees pay court
to Lungwort's

raspberry-pink blooms,
with blues and little moons.

10

"Isn't it splendid to think of all the things there are to find out about? It just makes me feel glad to be alive—it's such an interesting world. It wouldn't be half so interesting if we know all about everything, would it?"
—A.S.

My birthday star,

Tau Ceti, is 11.9
light years away.

Seen from the earth,
its brightness has
a magnitude of 3.5,
which is really
not very bright.

It moves across
the celestial sphere
in 2 arc seconds.

Its Latin name is
Tertia Struthionium
or Third of the Ostriches.

It is the Fifth
Star of Square Celestial.

You, however, shine
highest.

It would take some
time before
I reach you
at the tip
of the handle
that is Big Dipper's.

As you circle Polaris,

say, "*hey,*

North Star,

bright star,

stay right
where you are.

There, where she will
find you,
high and spry
in the Northern sky."

Wesley St. Jo

is the illustrator and co-author of *BLUE*, a whimsical poetry book launched at the Library of Congress in September 2017 and presented at the 4th Filipino American International Book Festival and at the San Francisco Litquake Festival in October 2017.

About Paloma Press

Established in 2016, **PALOMA PRESS** is an independent literary press publishing poetry, prose, and limited edition books. Titles include *BLUE* by Wesley St. Jo & Remé Grefalda, and *MANHATTAN: An Archaeology* by Eileen R. Tabios. Other releases include the fundraising chapbooks *MARAWI* and *AFTER IRMA AFTER HARVEY*. As part of the 2017 Litquake Festival in San Francisco, Paloma Press proudly curated the literary reading, "THREE SHEETS TO THE WIND."